BUCKEYES
A to Z

Mark Walter

illustrated by
Tim Williams

Buckeyes A to Z

Printed in the United States.

PRT0712C

ISBN-13: 978-1-936319-11-4
ISBN-10: 1-936319-11-X

Mascot Books
560 Herndon Parkway #120, Herndon, VA 20170

www.mascotbooks.com

For more books by Mark Walter or to contact the author visit
www.markwalterbooks.com or email info@markwalterbooks.com

Have a book idea? Contact us at:
Mascot Books
560 Herndon Parkway
Herndon, VA 20170
info@mascotbooks.com

Young Buckeye fans gather 'round,
Your learning tool has now been found.
You'll learn OSU facts from A to Z,
And become a Buckeye just like me.

Our greatest coach,
Was Woody Hayes.
Look for him,
On every page.

A is for Archie,
He wore 45.
A true Buckeye legend,
On the field he sure thrived.

Archie Griffin won the Heisman Trophy in 1974 and 1975. He is the only player to win the award two times.

The Ohio Buckeye (Aesculus glabra) became the official state tree in 1953. The tree received its name because the nut looks like a deer's eye.

B is for Buckeye,
The nickname and state tree.
And chocolate Buckeyes are delicious,
Just eat one and you'll see.

Woody Hayes was head coach at Ohio State from 1951 to 1978. His teams won national championships in 1954, 1957, 1961, 1968, and 1970. Jim Tressel, head coach from 2001 to 2011, led the Buckeyes to the national title in 2002. In 2011, Urban Meyer was named head coach.

C is for coaches,
Who work long days.
The Bucks have had legends,
Like Tressel and Hayes.

D is for dotting the "i,"
A tradition of the band.
Performed by a sousaphone player,
It's known across the land.

"Script Ohio" has been performed since
October 10, 1936. Sousaphone players
traditionally have the honor of dotting the "i."

E is for earning,
The famous Buckeye Leaf.
To place on a player's helmet,
After an excellent week.

One of Ohio State's most famous
traditions is awarding Buckeye Leaves
to players to wear on their helmets.
This tradition started in 1968.

Tim Williams

Ohio State's fight songs are the
"Buckeye Battle Cry" and "Across the Field."

F is for fans,
Who cheer the team along.
Together we'll sing,
The Buckeye fight song.

G is for George,
Number 27 he wore.
Winning the Heisman,
Put him in Buckeye lore.

Eddie George, a star running back for the Buckeyes
from 1992-1995, won the Heisman Trophy in 1995.

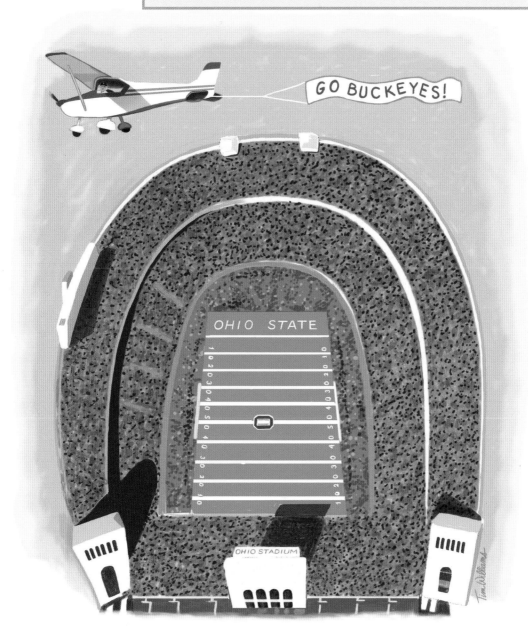

H is for Horseshoe,
A legend of its own.
This "U" shaped stadium,
Is where the Buckeyes call home.

I is for intensity,
The "Silver Bullets" play strong.
Stopping the offense,
Is their job all game long.

The Buckeye defense is often referred to as the "Silver Bullets." Defensive greats for the Buckeyes have included Mike Sensibaugh, Tom Cousineau, Marcus Marek, Luke Fickell, Mike Vrabel, Shawn Springs, Antoine Winfield, Nate Clements, and many others.

J is for jersey,
Made of scarlet and gray.
With hard work and practice,
You may wear one some day.

K is for kickers,
Greats like Janakievski and Nuuuuuuug,
3 points for a field goal,
When the ball goes up and through.

Mike Nugent was an All-American place kicker on the 2002 national championship team. Vlade Janakievski kicked for the Buckeyes from 1977-1980. He is a member of the Ohio State "All-Century Team."

L is for legends,
Players' dreams that came true.
Guys like Spielman, Laurinaitis, and Hawk,
Came alive in the 'Shoe.

Both Chris Spielman and A.J. Hawk were two-time All-Americans and won the Lombardi Award as the nation's top lineman (Spielman in 1987 and Hawk in 2005). James Laurinaitis was a three-time All-American, won the 2006 Nagurski Award as the nation's best defensive player, and won the 2007 Butkis Award as the nation's top linebacker.

Brutus Buckeye has been Ohio State's mascot since 1965. Brutus has gone through several appearance changes over the years after first being made of paper-mâché and weighing 40 pounds.

M is for mascot,
Brutus Buckeye's his name.
Leading our cheers,
He's at every game.

N is for national champs,
The prize for winning it all.
The Buckeyes have won many,
By playing great in the fall.

Ohio State won national championships
in 1942, 1954, 1957, 1961, 1968, 1970,
2002, _____, _____, _____.

Vic Janowicz (1950), Howard "Hopalong" Cassidy (1955), and Eddie George (1995) all won the Heisman Trophy. In addition, each player's jersey has been retired by Ohio State (Janowicz's #31, Cassidy's #40, and George's #27).

O is for offense,
Guys like Vic, Hop, and Eddie.
When it came time to play,
You knew they'd be ready.

P is for players,
On both sides of the ball.
Each one is important,
Juniors, seniors, and all.

In 2000, the Touchdown Club of Columbus selected Ohio State's "All-Century Team." It honors the greatest Buckeyes of the 20th century. Some of the members include Chic Harley, Les Horvath, Keith Byars, Cris Carter, Orlando Pace, Jack Tatum, Jim Stillwagon, and Jim Lachey.

Q is for quarterback,
A leader of the team.
Running the offense,
Is many kids' dream.

R is for rival,
Like the team from up North.
This fierce rivalry,
Goes back and forth.

Ohio State and Michigan first played in 1897. Each time the Buckeyes win, the coaches and players receive a miniature pair of gold pants symbolizing the victory.

S is for Senior Tackle,
A tradition built in the past.
During the final practice,
It's a memory that surely will last.

T is for Troy Smith,
A quarterback of the scarlet and gray.
His leadership and character,
Made him one of the best to this day.

Troy Smith led the Buckeyes to 3 straight victories over Michigan. He won the 2006 Heisman Trophy. Perhaps his greatest accomplishment is overcoming the many challenges he faced while growing up.

U is for university,
Ohio State's one of the best.
Since the year 1890,
Our team has risen above the rest.

V is for victory,
Let's go team, go.
And after our team wins,
We'll sing *Carmen Ohio*.

W is for Willis,
A true pioneer.
The All-American tackle,
Played with no fear.

Bill "Deke" Willis played for the Buckeyes from 1942-1944. He was the first African-American All-American at Ohio State.

X is for eXcellent,
A word for describing our band.
Two hundred twenty five members,
Make it "The Best in the Land."

The Ohio State Marching Band, also known as
"The Pride of the Buckeyes," usually performs its famous
"Script Ohio" before or during halftime of home games.

Y is for yelling,
Loud from the stands.
Cheers for the Buckeyes,
Heard from our great fans.

Z is for zzzzzzzz's,
You'll need sleep after you play.
Four quarters each game,
Makes for a mighty long day!

The Buckeye's have needed overtime for some of their greatest victories.
On their run to becoming the 2002 national champions, it took Ohio
State overtime to beat Illinois and double-overtime to beat Miami.

Way to go,
You've finished the book.
Next are some fun activities,
Just take a look...

Running Back Attack!

Pretend you are a running back. Roll the dice. That's how many yards you just gained. Keep track of your total number of yards to see how many you gained in one game. Each game consists of ten rolls per person. Also, you can double the amount of your last roll. Play a friend or family member. To make it harder, roll two or three dice at a time to see how many yards are gained per run.

For example:

First Roll = 6
Second Roll = 2
Third Roll = 3
Fourth Roll = 4
Fifth Roll = 6
Sixth Roll = 5
Seventh Roll = 2
Eighth Roll = 5
Ninth Roll = 3
Tenth Roll = 4 x 2 = 8

Total Yards Gained = 6 + 2 + 3 + 4 + 6 + 5 + 2 + 5 + 3 + 8 = 44 yards

Chocolate Buckeyes

Make this famous Buckeye treat for friends and family to enjoy on game day or any other time of the year.

Ingredients for Peanut Buttery Inside

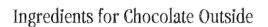

- 1 pound powdered sugar
- 1 1/4 sticks of butter, softened
- 12 oz. creamy peanut butter
- 1/2 tablespoon vanilla

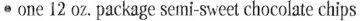

Ingredients for Chocolate Outside

- one 12 oz. package semi-sweet chocolate chips
- small amount of beeswax or paraffin (approximately 1/2 oz.)

Directions
- mix together the powdered sugar, softened butter, and vanilla
- add the peanut butter to the mixture (make sure the peanut butter is completely mixed in)
- roll mixture into Buckeye-sized balls (about 3/4" – 1" sized balls)
- refrigerate for two hours
- melt chocolate chips and beeswax or paraffin completely over a double boiler
- dip Buckeye balls into chocolate using a toothpick leaving a dime-sized circle of peanut butter showing at the top to resemble a Buckeye
- refrigerate or freeze
- serve and enjoy!

This recipe makes approximately 50-60 Buckeyes.

*Note – to get rid of the hole left by the toothpick, simply use the backside of a spoon rubbed in butter. Rub the spoon over the hole until it disappears.

Rhyme Time!

Locate the rhyming words on each page. See if you can come up with more rhyming words for each pattern.

<u>Example</u>
M is for mascot,
Brutus Buckeye's his name.
Leading our cheers,
He's at every game.

The word family pattern is –ame so here are a few words that fit:

- name
- game
- same
- fame

"Script Ohio"

The Ohio State Marching Band performs Script Ohio during home games. Pretend you are the drum major leading the band in this famous tradition by tracing the Script Ohio.

Ohio